This book is dedicated to all emotional support animals and the humans they love unconditionally.

Forever thankful to my parents, Amy & Dave, for their constant love & support.

ISBN: 9798851694936

“Today is the day I am going to find a forever home!” a tiny pup thought as she wriggled around in her pen. She had been at the shelter for three months hoping to be adopted by a loving family. No one had even glanced her way.

Yet, today was going to be different. She just knew it! Today, she would be home with a new name and sparkly collar.

Showing her value, she was on her best behavior compared to the other pups. She gave herself a quick splash in her water dish to look extra fluffy and adorable for when the doors opened that morning.

Hours ticked by, but still no owner.

Feeling discouraged, the little pup began to overthink. These thoughts made her whimper sadly as her big brown eyes filled with tears.

Meanwhile, fate had something special in store. A young girl named Marie was on her way to the shelter to browse the selection of precious pups. She was hopeful to find a furry friend to bring home.

You see, Marie was recently diagnosed with anxiety. Wanting to help, her parents learned about the benefits of emotional support animals. Knowing how much Marie loved dogs, a puppy was the perfect option.

Springing the door open to the shelter, Marie excitedly dashed over to the area of eager pups.

"That's the one!" Marie yelled with excitement.

The puppy yipped with utter excitement when the little girl pointed right at her.

"She's coming!"
"She's running right at me!"
"This is it! It's finally happening!"

Already in love, Marie scooped the miniature puppy into her arms...

...squeezed her tight, and never wanted to let go.

Marie loved everything about her new furry friend, even her big, pointy ears and crooked teeth. They reminded her of her own unique qualities. She also had large ears and funny teeth that crossed when she smiled.

"Beautiful! I am going to name you Bella," she squealed.

Bella had the best life a dog could dream of. She had a ginormous yard to run in, a beautiful house with a cozy bed, a colossal amount of toys, delicious food, and an entire pantry just for her treats! It was paradise.

However, as the days passed by, Bella noticed her human struggle. She often came home from school crying because she didn't feel like the other kids.

When this happened, Bella was always there to listen. She licked the salty tears off Marie's face as they rolled down her rosy cheeks. They tasted like delicious bones.

Marie worried about a lot of things. She wouldn't think about homework, toys, what to play with at recess, or what colored crayon to use on her art assignments.

Instead, she was secretly scared of
everything...even invisible germs!

In time, Bella was determined to help Marie conquer her fears. Bella would purposely leave a lot of accidents, loved getting into the pungent garbage, and would roll around in smelly stuff from outside. Although germs seemed scary to Marie, they weren't as bad as she originally thought. Germs were carefree and fun for a dog like Bella!

"Pew. You stink," Marie would say to Bella.
"Mission accomplished," barked Bella.

She also noticed Marie was afraid of losing the people she loved. Bella showed unconditional love and slept with her at night when her mind began to ponder. This made Marie feel comforted and safe before shutting her eyes to dream.

Although many children love to make messes, Marie loved a clean and organized environment. She often became agitated if her belongings weren't in order, but Bella was the opposite. She loved making big messes and scattering her toys around the house when playing. It would look like a toy store!

"This will teach her patience and that not everything always has to be in order," Bella thought. Marie realized that watching her new puppy play brought joy to her life.

Bella also noticed Marie would do the same things over and over again, like making sure she packed her lunch for school, brushing her teeth, or checking for imaginary monsters under her bed at night.

“Hmmm, that’s weird: she just checked for monsters under her bed. Why is she doing it again?” Bella questioned.

Bella reassured Marie by dragging pillows under her bed to show that no burly monster could fit under the tiny bed. After all, monsters were just fantasy creatures.

As days passed, Marie's parents noticed how much Bella was helping their daughter. She wasn't so fearful and anxious. She began to feel like an ordinary kid again.

Marie became a great caretaker for Bella too. She depended on her for things she couldn’t quite do on her own: making her breakfast and dinner, going on walks, vet visits, and cutting her fluffy hair. After all, she was just a puppy!

Now that Marie had to do so much for Bella, she forgot all about her own worries.

Marie's worries about germs, losing those she loved, organization, and imaginary monsters began to disappear. She focused more on what to draw with her favorite colored crayons, toys, and how to ace her homework. She even played during recess without a worry in the world!

When she came home from school, it was without tears trickling down her face. She was greeted by one cheerful puppy ready to pounce on her with kisses.

Marie realized how much Bella helped by staying at her side, cheering her up with her wagging tail and goofy antics. Bella was the one who made it all happen with her loyal companionship. Yet, Bella was overjoyed to have a loving owner who treated her like royalty.

Although Bella had been waiting for a family to adopt her, she realized Marie needed her just as much. Bella and Marie became best friends and loyal companions.

“I love you, Bella. You are my best friend,” Marie whispered as she hugged her furry companion.

Bella wagged her tail, snuggled into Marie’s heart, and thought, “And you are mine.”

Thank you for picking up this book & taking the time to read it. If you are unfamiliar with anxiety or emotional support animals, here's just a glimpse into their meaning and benefits.

What is Anxiety?

According to Mayo Clinic, people with anxiety disorders frequently have intense, excessive, and persistent worry or fear about everyday situations. Although occasional anxiety is normal, anxiety disorders interfere with daily activities, are difficult to control, are out of proportion to actual danger, and can last a long time. Symptoms can start during childhood, teen years and continue into adulthood. To learn more, visit mayoclinic.org or seek a medical professional.

Animals for Mental Health

Emotional Support Animals may help alleviate the symptoms of multiple conditions. These include providing help with depression, anxiety, and other social disorders. Caring for animals is extremely beneficial in many ways. According to the Mental Health Foundation of the United Kingdom, animals provide companionship, give a sense of security, can reduce anxiety by boosting self-confidence, provide unconditional love, add structure to your day, and increase physical activity to boost your overall mood. The National Alliance on Mental Illness also stated, "People with dogs have lower blood pressure and are less likely to develop heart disease—just playing with dogs has been shown to elevate oxytocin and dopamine, creating positive feelings and bonding for both the person and their pet." However, dogs aren't the only pets that have power over our mental well-being. Other pets like cats, ferrets, horses, birds, and even fish have a role in mental health. For people with a mental health condition, research has shown that time with pets reduces anxiety levels more than other recreational activities (NAMI). Pretty amazing! If you are thinking of adopting a pet, please do your research and understand that animals are a lifelong commitment! It is truly a symbiotic relationship leading to one of the greatest companionships you'll ever know— just like Marie & Bella's!

Sources

Mayo Clinic Staff. (n.d.). Anxiety Disorders. Mayo Clinic, https://www.mayoclinic.org/diseases-conditions/anxiety/symptoms-causes/syc-20350961.3/15/2023

Pets and mental health. (2022, February 15). Mental Health Foundation. https://www.mentalhealth.org.uk/explore-mental-health/a-z-topics/pets-and-mental-health#:~:text=The%20companionship%20of%20a%20pet,you%20feel%20isolated%

How pets can help us maintain mental health. (2020, August 26). NAMI California. https://namica.org/blog/how-dogs-can-help-us-maintain-mental-health/

www.ingramcontent.com/pod-product-compliance
Lightning Source LLC
Chambersburg PA
CBHW041739040625
27697CB00039B/11

* 9 7 9 8 8 5 1 6 9 4 9 3 6 *